THE

EDGE

OF

BANKCRUPTCY

A Survivor's Guide
to Battling Back
from the Brink of
Business Disaster

Peter Rollo MBA and Yogeeta Devi CA MBA

Printed by Peter Rollo, in the United States of America.

First printing, 2020.

Publisher

Peter Rollo
62 Bell Street, Kawerau
Bay of Plenty
New Zealand
3127

Website: peterrollo.biz

Summary: The perfect book for an imperfect world! In these troubled times, author Peter Rollo delivers a must-read guide to battling back from the brink of business disaster. He shares his perilous journey to avoid bankruptcy during the Global Financial Crisis of 2008 and gives readers analysis, insight, and point-by-point instruction to keep their own businesses afloat during the toughest of times. Full of first-hand accounts and savvy advice, it's a must-read for small-and-medium business owners as they battle the next global recession and beyond.

A must read for any business owner or manager experiencing a cash flow crunch. In fact, this is a must read for **anybody** in business because black swan events do happen and can sneak up on your business like the perfect storm. I have wanted to write this book for a long time, and with the coronavirus ravaging the world's economy and forcing us all to work remotely, I decided it was time to get focused, sit down and write out my experiences, my painful and powerful lessons learned, and how you can take my knowledge to guide you through any business pitfall.

What is a Black Swan?

Like the bird of the same name, a black swan is an unpredictable event, often a force of nature, that goes beyond the normal expectations of a situation, resulting in catastrophic events. While they don't occur often, people are rarely prepared to deal with them, despite the fact that when the effects have passed, many will say it was obvious they were imminent.

CONTENTS

Introduction

My name is Peter Rollo and I'm a native of New Zealand. I became a small business owner in the early 2000s and was able to not only survive the last Global Financial Crisis (GFC) that began in 2007 and lasted to 2009, but also come out stronger on the other side, eventually making millions in profits. Today, I am semi-retired at the age of 41, and my partner and I are plotting a trip around the world via a large sailing catamaran we recently purchased. That introduction probably sounds like one of the "get-rich-quick" schemes you see on late-night television or via spam mail that slips past your virus protector and into your inbox. However, I am not here to sell you any sort of method, technique, 12-step program, or magic pill; I deal solely in the facts.

I am not a fancy consultant or the CEO of a big corporation. I am a practical business owner who has been on the front lines and experienced first-hand what it is like to make tough decisions to stay in business. When the GFC happened, I was about as insolvent as a dog turd and had no secret benefactor or trust fund to bail me out. If I was unable to turn the business around, I would be bankrupt and probably would have owed $200,000 or more in debts all over town.

I'm going to tell you my story - the good and the bad; the fist-punching highs and the emotionally-draining lows. Then I'm going to share with you how I got out of it, how I got better, and how you can do the exact same thing. There is no quick-fix solution to a small business that is in trouble; no magic pill you can swallow that turns a cash-flow crisis into a waterfall of currency. If you read enough business books, you start to notice that they all start sounding quite a bit alike. In the first part you're told what you're doing wrong. In the second part you're given a series of steps that are supposedly "one size fits all", and in the third part you're patting yourself on the back and so filthy rich that you don't mind forking over $39.95 to the author of the book in exchange for their brilliant advice.

The problem with a lot of those books is that they are being written by people who have never been where I was and where you very well might be right now. As I write this, it appears the world is slowly tilting back towards normalcy from the greatest economic disruption since the GFC: the coronavirus. In the last century, our small businesses have faced violence and volatility, hurricanes and floods and earthquakes, but never once could we have imagined a crisis where our stores closed and stayed closed for weeks on end in an effort to combat a virus from sweeping across the globe and killing millions.

You name it and I have faced it, solving dozens of small-to-medium business (SMB) problems from cash flow crises to employing staff to restructuring to re-negotiating my leases. I have been there. Because I could not pay I rang the landlord and tax men and sacked members of my staff. I didn't take these decisions lightly. I did anything I could to pay my bills and save my employees' jobs; they were great people who became much more than employees over time. The downturn and the decisions that followed cause me considerable pain. I spent many nights at home in tears wondering how I could possibly turn the situation around. My business was very well known in the town I lived in, so you can imagine the embarrassment it brought to me and my family as I teetered on the verge of bankruptcy.

Like other Kiwis have in the past, I could have run and hidden in another country, probably Australia. However, owning my own business and being my own boss had long been my dreams. I didn't become an entrepreneur just to give up the first time something failed. That's the polar opposite of what the spirit of entrepreneurship is all about. I found that I had some fight in me and I was not yet booking airline tickets. The fact that I had just broken up with my long-term girlfriend did not help things either, but it did give me a great conduit to focus my thoughts and energy on the problem I could fix, not the one where the damage was already done and now irreversible. Honestly, at some point I just figured, what else could go wrong?

The path to success is not a straight line, and as business owners, we can expect to encounter many challenges along the way. But how you react to those challenges and how you pick yourself up and keep on going will determine your success. Throughout this book, I have shared my experiences and with the help from my partner, who is an accountant for small businesses, we have provided tools and practical guidelines which will help you in times of crises like during this coronavirus pandemic. Some of the decisions we discuss here will push you out of your comfort zone. Desperate times call for desperate measures, right?

Chapter 1:

My Story

I started my first business at age 2 (no really!) and I have always had that passion to get into the business world and be my own boss, make the decisions, all of that stuff. I worked for my dad on the family farm at an hourly rate and I was always very business focused. I was out of high school when I started working as a butcher. Was I the best butcher in the world? I think it's safe to say I was not, but that was OK because I really was not focused on cutting meat. I was fascinated with the behind-the-scenes stuff and I started managing the books and taking care of the shop's bills after working there only a few months. That's where I started learning about business - on the job. By the time I was 18 or 19, I was doing the ordering for the supermarket and the merchandising as well.

In 2001 at the age of 22, I started a car auction business with $30,000. My parents helped me out at the beginning and I got the auction started by selling cars on behalf of people and charging a commission so I did not have to fund the stock myself. I managed to find a motivated landlord who was willing to give me a few rent free periods, and $45,000 cash for my start-up. You see it was a new subdivision being built and they needed businesses to fill it out. It worked out well, so I signed a lease, put up some signs, ordered the prerequisite desks and chairs, and made it official with a few staffers. We were in business! Back in those days you had to have a dealers' license if you were going to sell cars in New Zealand, so I worked around that by taking people's cars and auctioning them. I'd sell cars on behalf of other people and charge them a commission. I was about to turn 22 and was already running my own business; I mean really living the dream! Of course that dream turned into a nightmare within about six weeks' time because like most businesses, I really struggled early on. I didn't have a lot of profit margin, and my cash flow was very tight. I had very little income week to week and by the end of the first week, I had more than $30,000 in bills! I just couldn't believe I had accrued so much debt in such a short period of time.

I can remember being at home in tears after the first auction sale with maybe one car sold and little income and mounting debts. I remember a few weeks into it adding up all the bills and going, *"Holy shit, how can I owe that much?*

But I kept going, because when you're 22 and an entrepreneur, what else can you do? No one was going to convince me that it was a bad idea or that I was in over my head. I started looking for cars anywhere I could find them. Mechanics were giving me a break and not charging me for repairs until I could pay for them, sometimes not until a year later. I started making calls to private owners and telling them I could sell their cars much better than at a lot, and that started picking up the business. After doing that for a while, the dealerships themselves started coming to me with trade-ins in order to get them sold for as much money as possible.

Ever so slowly the sales started building up and we were turning a profit. Now the goal was to franchise the business, so profits were being spent on franchise preparation, branding, and legal. That meant we were not retaining a lot of these profits. Or put another way, we were not saving for a rainy day. The real boom started for me in 2002 and lasted until about 2006. We had very big growth in those times. I remember having sold 30 cars in just one auction and we'd put on a free barbecue so people would show up, and then we would get to work on selling the cars. In 2006, the industry started getting really competitive, and when that happens, you're going to start falling off. I had not retained a lot of profits as I was trying to make it a franchise all over the country and trying to turn my business into a corporation.

In 2007, my dad, who was always amazing about offering advice but not telling me what to do, mentioned something to me about the economic unrest in America. I blew it off because I lived in New Zealand and was only selling cars, what did the US economy have to do with me? If I had been paying attention to the world beyond my own business and bank account, the answer to that would have been "EVERYTHING." I realize many people reading this book were still growing up in 2007 (a terrible thought to someone my age!) and that things like the coronavirus have taken center stage lately, so let's review what happened during that time and what it meant for a business like mine.

Chapter 2:

Learn History So As Not to Repeat History

The Great Recession did not happen because of just one thing, but it did take the form of a full-fledged black swan event as is described and defined in the opening of this book. It was the worst economic crisis the world has faced since the Great Depression of the 1930s, which only ended when every country in the world started declaring war on one another.

The Great Recession actually got its start as far back as 2005 when the US housing bubble burst. In an act of nearly unparalleled greed, mortgage lender banks were approving just about everyone for a loan for a few years. Many of these banks made even more of a killing by selling and reselling the loans to other banks. The more loans you gave out, the more you could make by selling them to other companies. Even Americans who had nowhere near the income or income-to-debt ratio were being approved for houses way outside their affordability range.

Within a year or two, thousands of these new-loan home owners were defaulting on payments and falling into foreclosure situations. This affected American interest rates, available credit, hedge funds, and multiple foreign bank markets. In October of 2007, probably about the time my dad was trying to warn me of the impending tidal wave, the US Secretary of the Treasury called the busted bubble the biggest risk to the US economy.

I was in my late 20s and had my head buried in the sand. In fact in early 2008, I took an extended holiday with no idea that a devastating reduction in turnover was waiting for me when I returned. I got back and things were bad. I had been in business for nine years and had taken the long hard slog, starting from almost nothing. My dad's words were ringing in my ears when I got back to find sales non-existent in February 2008. On the other side of the world, Americans were defaulting on mortgage payments left and right and walking away from those loans. The American housing market sunk like a stone. Without their mortgage payments, US banks could no longer loan money to small businesses and the like. American private citizens stopped spending and started using their income to pay down debt. The country was screeching to a very loud halt.

As the biggest economy in the world, when something major happens in the US, it affects the rest of the world. You know how when you toss a stone into a still lake it creates ripples that will move all the way to the shore? The housing bubble bursting in the US was like someone chunking a boulder into that lake. Its ripples were like huge waves crashing outward towards the rest of the world. Most of North America, South America, and the EU fell into recessions of their own based on their strong ties to the US economy.

You see recessions or financial crises come every 5-9 years. Between these years, people start-up businesses and/or join the workforce without experiencing the bad stuff. They have experienced high business growth, pay rises, and their business confidence is naïve about the dramatic effect these events can have on both the business and their personal lives. They have never experienced a recession or financial crises. And if you haven't experienced times of crises, then how can you be prepared?

Since I had been putting away money in savings for other endeavours for a while, I was more prepared than some might have been. I had built up some cash during the year because of small talk I had heard of a coming recession, but nothing like what happened in the US. If I hadn't done this one thing with the cash, I think my business might have failed completely. That would have been bad enough for me, but by that point my parents were retiring and owned some shares in the company. Their major source of income was my business being successful. If it failed, they would have no money coming in. The motivation to work for both myself and my family kicked in when I was teetering on the brink and got me brainstorming to figure out a way to fight through it. I'll never know for sure, but if it was just me, I might have been very tempted just to lock the front gate and run away. But that's the power of purpose: What will keep you going in really difficult times?

It really hit me that things were falling apart in December 2007. It was tough on everyone. On top of that, suddenly every business you had an outstanding invoice with wanted their money. My accountant had been advising me to grow for some time. He had been encouraging me to grow, so all our spare cash went on growth and not retaining profits. So even though I had been receiving professional accounting advice I was still trading from an insolvent balance sheet before the recession started. An insolvent balance sheet means not enough savings for a rainy day, or put another way, it was a business that lived from week to week. I knew I was going to be in a cashflow hole for 3-8 months, and that meant things were going to be very difficult for the business and very bad for myself and my employees.

There was a certain disbelief to all of it. I had been in business for almost a decade and things were on an upward trend after a rough start. Suddenly there were tons of cars and no customers. You decide you can get through it by doing your normal routine plus a few extra things. I mean that's always worked in the past, right? You're the boss and you like to think you are in control of everything and can pull all the strings. But the reality is that there are some things you simply cannot control no matter if you're you, me, Warren Buffett, Bill Gates, or anyone else.

Sometimes the economy is going to take a dive, and if you are not prepared, you will be swept out to sea.

So I did the normal things that you do when business is sluggish. I got my "natural born leader" face on and started motivating my staff to sell more, beat the bushes, and find those customers who are willing to buy under any circumstances. I followed up personally with more customers, the way you do when you're the one who used to be a salesman and now you're running the whole show. You're always convinced you're going to succeed where your employees are struggling because you're YOU, and you're the one who got this whole thing going in the first place. When things continued to be sluggish, I started stretching out my bill pay cycles. You don't have to always pay every single bill as it comes. You can get them in cycles of 30 and 60 and 90 days, but at 90 days things turn into a big mess because once you go past that mark, the places you owe can turn you over to a collection agency, which can wreak havoc on your credit score. Against my better judgement, I had to start reducing staff. That's tough too, because people are more than just employees after a while, they become your friends and to a large degree your family. You see them every day. Your successes are their successes and your failures are their failures.

That made it even harder when it came to redundancies. It's difficult because at some point you have to use them. I had to do that to a few part-timers and they were people who were good workers and really valuable members of the company. One lady was an expert at putting together systems and structure, but I had to let her go. We're still friends on Facebook, but it really hurt.

You have to make some horrible decisions. The Britney Spears song "Piece of Me' was out then and it always reminds me of how I felt back then. One guy in particular I really wanted to keep on, and he was so generous and amazing during the process. He told me he had some personal stuff that he could sell to stay afloat. So we tried to cut costs and grow sales, because what else can you do?

We struggled to get the cashflow back to positive. From December 2007 to May 2008 we failed to do that. That's six months without seeing a profit. Of course at the same time I was going through a rough breakup with my girlfriend who was also working for me at the time. That relationship was going to fall apart anyway, but the financial disaster sped it up and made the fracture grow wider. I kept my parents at the top of mind every time I thought about quitting. They had put up money at the start of the business to help me get going, I couldn't let them down now. I struggled with depression through all of this. I remember a time when I went water skiing on my little boat one summer and laughed, and it felt like it was the first time I had laughed in two years.

In May 2008, we broke even. It felt like winning the lottery. In June, we made a few thousand dollars in profit. It felt incredible. I was determined to never get that close to the edge again so I started really saving my money and being very smart about how I was running things. I lived in a very small flat and took on some flatmates to make it even more affordable. Even some of my co-workers were wondering why I was living in such a small place, but flat rates were very cheap and it was a great way to save money. I was barely there anyway. I saved that money to build the business up, and we moved the business model from a car auction to a paper auction. Then around 2013-2014 it became a high volume used car dealership. I was pivoting the business model to keep growing.

I was saving tons and making sound investments. I bought a $200,000 boat in 2016 and paid off my mortgage. That was just seven years after being at the brink of bankruptcy. By then, I knew it was time to get out, as there was too much competition. I got out of the business in 2018. Now I own my house and my catamaran outright. I feel great about how I got here and want to share it with people who are where I was. I've experienced the pain that a lot of you are going through or have gone through, and I realized that the best thing I could do was share that information with others to give them a chance to avoid falling into the same trap. That's where the idea for this book first began to germinate. I got out of the car dealing business and became a business consultant and a teacher.

I have come to realize firstly from experience and secondly from study that economics travels in cycles that you could best describe as first being on a rocketship and then holding onto a parachute. When the rocketship is blasting off and getting up to its maximum speed, you feel like you'll never stop making money and expanding your base. It feels like everyone wants to buy from you and everyone knows your name. But if you know anything about business, economics, or heck even how a rocket works, you have to realize that at some point it's going to run out of fuel and you're going to come crashing back down to earth. If you don't have the parachute on your back when that downfall happens, the drop is liable to kill your business and put you into the poor house. Even having the best parachute in the world isn't going to make you bullet-proof. Imagine taking a rocket ship that launches from your house and gets just out of the Earth's atmosphere to the point where the sky stops being earth blue and turns into the black of space. Now imagine at that exact moment, you run out of fuel and the rocketship starts to turn down. You could stay in it, I suppose, and crash to the ground with it. Not much chance of survival there, but at least you'd be remembered as the captain who went down with the ship. Alternatively, you could have an escape plan in mind thanks to that parachute on your back. You bail out, but it's still a long way back down to your house with all sorts of difficulties to overcome along the way. You navigate it the best you can, but you're surely going to hit some rough patches of air and struggle to stay on course. But as long as you can land with both feet on the ground, you're still in the game and have a chance to build your business back up.

So that's a brief look at my story. That's how I went from chopping meat at a butcher's shop to flying high with my car auction business. The global recession sent me crashing back down to earth, but I was able to keep my head in the game and ride out the storm thanks to my cash flow, my hard work, and let's face it, a whole lot of luck. Now that you know how I got to where I am, I'm going to help you get where you want to go.

To make it as easy to read as possible, we have divided this book into key sections like cash flow, revising your business plan, marketing, etc. In each section we will touch base with my story and what I did to survive in business, followed by a notes section for you to reflect and make plans for your business. We have provided a guidelines/ to-do list at the end of each section which should help you make some smart decisions to turn your business around.

Chapter 3:

The Importance of Cash

Have you ever heard the phrase the calm before the storm? When you're sailing on the ocean, it's that lull in the weather before the clouds roll in, the waves start rocking, and the rain starts pouring down on you. It's an eerie feeling, but if you are not really paying attention, you might miss it completely. But you'll soon realize what's going on as you are blown away when the hurricane or typhoon springs to life around you and starts ripping your vessel to shreds.

If you're paying attention, you will know when things have shifted in the economy. The bookings get cancelled, the phone stops ringing, and your staff is all standing around. It might seem like a quiet day, we all have those, but then it becomes a week or two, and then it becomes the new normal. Economic conditions are changing with a reduction in consumer spending. No matter what business you are in, you're going to experience it. When the Global Financial Crisis was at its peak, my gross income dropped by 30-50%. No matter what I did, nothing seemed to work to increase sales. That's a very tough feeling, and a very uncomfortable one. Natural born salespeople feel like they could sell ice to a penguin on Christmas morning in Antarctica if it came right down to it. When you're seeing no money coming through the door, and customers you used to count on are now not returning your calls or telling you that their budgets are just too tight, you begin to get a sense that something bigger is at play. At the time of the Global

Financial Crisis my cash flow was already tight, as I had been spending money for years investing it both in branding and in systems as we were improving the business for potential franchising all over the country.

We were zipping our way through five years of growth, and it made sense at the time to start turning those profits into work for future investments. The company was going to get so much bigger in a few years, it was the ideal situation until it suddenly was not. So what did I do when revenue stopped rolling in and my cash flow grew even tighter?

First and foremost, I took over my company's job of paying bills and managing the cash flow from the lady who was the administrator of that area. She was doing a perfect job for boom time, but we were no longer there. She also nearly destroyed my cashflow by paying too many bills as soon as she opened the envelopes each week. But I knew who my vendors were and who my suppliers were and how much leeway I had with all my bills, so I took over the spot and started to manage them as shrewdly and smartly as I could. As I mentioned earlier, there are plenty of bills that come in on a 30-day cycle, but you're not going to start getting penalized for them until that cycle goes past 90 days. So that's a three-month opening between the day you get the bill and the day you absolutely have to pay it before you get referred to collections and your credit score takes a hit. Remember, credit is great, but cash is better. In the short term of a financial crisis, you have to keep some cash on hand because you still need to live. If you don't have enough in the bank to pay the rent at your store this month or the cost of getting the cars at our auction house repaired, those are clearly bills that can wait and will come around again in 30 days, and again in another 60 days. But if you have no cash on hand, how can you buy food from the grocery store? Or pay for petrol to fill up your vehicle? If you run out of cash, you're dead in the water. They'll cut off your data service on your phone and you'll literally be stuck.

When the Global Financial Crisis occurred, I switched into survival mode with my creditors. I made contact with them early on and let them know what was going on in my world and that I was prepared to pay them back, but it was not going to be in the normal, formal way that we had been carrying on to date. Instead, I made payment arrangements for small weekly amounts. I struck while the iron was hot instead of waiting for them to call or start harassing me for funds. On the whole suppliers were supportive because they know if businesses are not selling merchandise, they have no money to pay the bills. It's just like what we've seen in 2020 with the shuttering of entire countries for "social distancing" during the COVID-19 epidemic. Everyone agrees we're keeping a lot more people safe and healthy by having all "non-essential" businesses close down, but eventually you run into the brick wall where stores with no customers cannot make any money, thus becoming unable to pay their bills. Customers have no disposable income because their jobs are largely shut down, and before you know it we're in a recession that makes the previous one feel like we just forgot our lunch money on the way to school.

Of course, my monthly bills were not my only expenses at the time. I can very vividly remember the day I got in my car and drove from place to place all over town to see my suppliers. I had been that brash guy early in my business career - you know, the 20-something year-old with the booming business - and now here I was having to go to them and tell them that I could not pay my business expenses at the present time, except for given amounts at certain times.

Doing this upfront was probably my saving grace. Think how much time and effort businesses have to spend chasing down people who don't pay their bills, with the knowledge that some of the people will spend the rest of their days ignoring the payments they owe. That's really disheartening for any business to endure. I didn't want them to think I was not good for the money because once they start calling you wanting to get paid, they're going to be a lot less agreeable on terms that are favorable to you. If you're the one who approaches them, however, you're giving them the indication that you're a person who believes in paying their debts regardless of their financial constraints. The same is true for you if you're struggling to pay your taxes. If you know you can't pay the full amount by tax day, call your local or federal tax office and let them know about it before the fact. That's the best way to get them to work with you. I made my bed and now I had to lay in it, and you will have to do the same, but remember it's just a short-term strategy to keep your business afloat.

Long term you can't rely on not paying your bills to run your business no matter how nice suppliers are. I sat down 2-3 times a week and went through my suppliers' list and prioritised what amount and who to pay. I was in complete control of this process, not my administration assistant, because I was the only one with enough knowledge to make everything click. You'll be the same if you encounter this problem, because you are the only person who has that entire top-down view of your business. If you don't have that view, you've got problems. You should be the one who knows everything about what's going in and what's coming out of your business.

I was making sure the most vital suppliers were getting paid every week, even if it was a small amount. To be honest, some of the ones that were not as crucial I was stringing out a bit more. Losing those would not have been as crushing a blow, and I was trying to keep the best parts of my business intact. I had to prioritise no matter how uncomfortable I might have felt about it.

Chapter 4:

A New Budget for a New Reality

When you are in business, you're making a budget every month based on how much you're planning on spending and how much you're planning on making. These estimates are based on your data analysis, economic indicators, and whatever else you might build your specific estimates on. When times of financial struggle crop up, that budget goes right out the window, or at least to the back of the drawer until things get better. What you did last month, or trying to compare your revenue year over year, doesn't work now. You've got to make a new budget based on the amount of sales you think you can maintain in a worst-case scenario.

How does that work? Well, you'll need to play devil's advocate to make it happen. If you grossed $10,000 in sales in January, $8,000 in February, and $7,000 in March, you'll have to assume that things aren't quite done taking a dip. You should definitely be checking the financial reports - online, on TV, wherever you get your news - to see what sort of indicators there are going forward. How's your country's currency doing against the US dollar and the euro? What's your federal interest rate doing? Are people spending more on goods and services or more on paying down debt? You have to know big-picture stuff in order to estimate how your company fits in the mix.

As for your worst-case scenario, take a good look at those factors and combine them with any knowledge you have of your long-term or repeat customers. Now the ultimate worst-case scenario might be that they all go out of business, but that's a bit extreme. Envision what your budget would be like if you lost 50% of their business, or if a few dropped out entirely. If you already have contracts in place through the following month, you can include that in your expected income; unless something is giving you pause due to the communication with said customers that tells you otherwise.

When I did my new budget, I saw that I needed to cut costs below my new projected gross income levels. It would take reducing a ton of overhead, but if I could do it, I could still make a profit of $60,000-$70,000 per year.

But making a budget and adhering to a budget are two very different things. For starters, a lot of the sacrifices I was making were not on the business end, but on the personal end - which meant taking away some of my creature comforts to stretch each dollar. That's when I downgraded my residence and took on some flatmates. What a huge reduction in cost that was! Reducing your cost of living is an amazing way to stay ahead on your cash flow. Even my bankers were surprised to find out how cheaply I was living. Speaking of bankers, they were the only ones not willing to work with me on making smaller weekly payments instead of my big monthly ones. This is not meant to be an indictment of banks or bankers, but more of a warning: If you run into a bunch of debt, unpaid bills, or negative cash flow, make sure you pay your bank loans. Their entire business is money, and they usually aren't as flexible about smaller amounts of recompensation.

"If turnover is vanity, and profit is sanity, then cash is king for your business"

"You will be dead like a dried up 50 year old rat found in the wall of a house during a renovation project if you run out of cash. Cash is your blood and gives you room to manoeuvre and save yourself"

"Better to steer the ship then to run or hide. Humans tend to go through the flight-or-fight reaction when things get tough. How do you handle things when the rubber meets the road, have you got the spine to do what it takes to survive in the business? Or are you going to bury your head in the sand and blame the circumstances?"

"Add up how much spare cash you have. Make partial payments (e.g. if you owe $1,000, only pay $100, give the person warning and ask for help. They won't like it but what can they really do? All this does is buy you time. It's still a debt you will owe and when you come back better than ever you can pay them back"

Chapter 5:

Have An Escape Plan

I'd been making savings to an account in my mum's name to keep it safe from my business risks and it had about NZ$7,000 in it. My dad asked if I wanted to put this into the business. My response? HELL NO! That $7,000 was my lifeline, my last line of defence if things should get really bad. As a lot of small business owners are finding out during the coronavirus pandemic of 2020, at some point you have to put your family, your life, and your health ahead of everything else. Your business is important. For some people it feels like their entire life, but it is not. If your business was shut down for an extended period of time by COVID-19, you no doubt felt a lot of pressure to continue paying your employees, your suppliers, your utility bills, your mortgage, etc. But at some point when no money is coming in, you can't keep sending money out the door. Nobody can. Not even the likes of Warren Buffett or Richard Branson. Heck, even professional sports teams are cutting off their athletes' salaries as I am writing this, and really, can you blame them? Just because a team in the NFL or the NBA is worth hundreds of millions, or even billions, doesn't mean they've got a secret waterfall that rains cash down 24 hours a day. Those big franchises rely on TV money, ticket sales, and merchandising. There's no TV money when there are no games on TV, and nobody is buying tickets for something they can't go to. It also affects the season tickets that people buy in advance. Those aren't even being offered by the teams, because nobody knows when the next season of sports anywhere on the globe is going to start. And when people are pinching their pennies to take care of their own homes, you can bet they're not spending them on sports jerseys and autographed soccer balls.

So that $7,000 account was like my own private little gold mine. If I put all $7,000 of it into a business venture - say increased advertising, or paid my employees for another month before I had to start the redundancies or the layoffs, then what would I do when that time period ended? Even if I really used my head and spread it around everywhere: some to my employees, some to my landlord, some to the radio station for a few more spots, these would all be small amounts of money that might not actually do anything to improve the situation. It came down to not only a matter of sheer survival for me, but also the ability to understand that the solution in hand was not going to fix the problem.

Say you're a new business and you put together a radio spot that brought in 20 new customers, and your revenue doubled for a month. Three months later, you're nearly out of cash and haven't been able to afford another radio spot so you're getting desperate about what to do. The economy is OK, you're just struggling through growing pains like all businesses do. In that instance, taking something from a savings account like I had would be an acceptable risk, because you have hard data backing you up that this strategy has worked before, and more importantly, there are no outside factors that would inhibit it from working again. In my situation during the Global Financial Crisis, even if I used that $7,000 to invoke a strategy that had worked brilliantly before - say an email campaign or a billboard on a well-travelled highway - it still would have had little-to-no effect on the situation because my brand exposure was not the problem. The problem was that we were in a recession, and instead of buying cars, people were saving their money, spending it on essentials, and paying down their debt. In that environment, spending money on a radio ad made no sense. If you are feeling chilly in your house, you might make a cup of tea or hot chocolate to warm you up. But if you first need to walk three miles to the grocery store and it's snowing outside, as good as that drink might warm you up on the inside, once you're outside that door, you're going to be freezing cold very quickly.

The comfort this $7,000 brought was immeasurable and probably helped me have the energy to save the business. If my turnaround failed, this was my fund to pay my rent and buy groceries and live for a month or two to clear my head and fly somewhere to find a job. Failing in a very public way at a business after 9 years of running it would be a massive personal crisis to go through. If you also can't buy your groceries and have to move into a friend's house with mere cents to your name, I think it would be a much darker personal tragedy.

As it was, my mental health suffered, and I'm not afraid to open up and admit it, because most business books won't go into that part of what it takes to run and maintain a small business. As an entrepreneur, you might be the type of person who comes bouncing out of bed every morning singing a song and ready to conquer the world with a smile on your face. But even that sort of personality can be affected by something like a recession and the prospect of losing the thing you've worked so hard and put so much time, money, and energy into. About the only thing I can equate it to, is if you had spent years building your own house on your own plot of land, and now a wildfire had broken out and it was burning its way right towards your house. You could see it coming and get yourself and your family out, maybe even save a few meagre possessions. But there was no doubt that this fire was going to destroy everything you had worked for and spent a decade building. The Global Financial Crisis was an inferno of a different kind, and even though it had been kindled in the United States, it was blazing its way across New Zealand and just about every other country in the world. Depression makes life much more difficult. Simple tasks seem tough and complex tasks seem impossible. The 'bounce out of bed' feeling recedes and the 'why bother' feeling starts to press on your heart and your mind. A big part of being an entrepreneur and a small-business owner is the mentality that there's no problem you cannot fix, no sale you cannot close.

One of my favorite all-time anecdotes about another entrepreneur comes from American history and Thomas Edison, widely regarded as the father of modern electricity. When he debuted his world-changing incandescent lightbulb to the world in December 1879, he was asked by a newspaper reporter if the rumour was true that he had suffered through 10,000 failed experiments before being successful. Edison famously quipped that he had not failed 10,000 times, he had discovered 10,000 ways to not make a lightbulb, all of which led him to the one way to make one. That might be how you've felt if you've ever had to start and stop and start again with your business. Eventually, all your misfires get you to the point you are now where you've got a small business, you've made some sales, found some customers, but now you're struggling. If you were in business during the Global Financial Crisis or you're battling your way through the COVID-19 pandemic, it can feel like you've built yourself the perfect little world only to have a giant come step on it and crush it with his foot. In such a scenario, you could try asking him to move, giving him a hot foot, poking him with a letter opener, but none of it is effective: he is simply too big. In some cases, you have to make the adjustments to your own little world to survive until the giant moves on.

Credit conditions tightened significantly during the Global Financial Crisis. I had a bank line of credit with which to buy stock. I expected the bank would take this credit away, so I had to look for an alternative. I eventually found one, although the search process was not easy and the terms were less than favorable. But what mattered is that I found someone who was willing to lend me money so I could continue to buy cars to put up for auction - which was the only way we were going to make any money and start climbing out of this hole. Guess what? After a few months, I got the letter in the mail from the bank that I had been expecting. My line of credit had been withdrawn. Many of my competitors got them on the exact same day, but there was one major difference among us. Many of them had simply stood around worrying about the problem, while I had gone out and been proactive, much as I had been with my suppliers at the beginning of this chapter.

Many guys lost their car yards by not being able to secure alternative financing. The interesting thing was that after a further six months of operating, I was making good profits and was able to save money for stock. Even though there was no further need to maintain that line of credit, I still had some. By significantly cutting my own cost of living, I had more money to spend as things started working their way back to normal, while the competition was still struggling to find money to buy new inventory.

Planning ahead is an incredible weapon when things start to get stagnant. Business owners are usually very hard workers, but we all know there is a tremendous difference between working hard and working smart. When I was running around town talking to my suppliers about how I was going to pay them and finding an alternative line of credit, a lot of guys in my industry were trying to bash their way out of the problem by spending more money to generate more interest. When it didn't work, they were out the money they had spent with no return on investment. That's about the worst 1-2 combination you can have. That's the sort of environment where bankruptcy happens.

Chapter 6:

Playing Hardball

Like I mentioned before, there are some people who are not going to work with you when things go bad. I had that problem with the banks and other people will have it with their landlords. If you ask for a grace period or a rent reduction, you have to consider the problem from the landlord's point of view because this can help you negotiate your way through it. You might have to risk breaking your contract with the landlord because you can only pay what you can pay. If that's not going to work, you might end up taking your business online or moving it into your garage in the short term. You'll need to have completed the budget we talked about earlier before you go to speak to your landlord, or possibly better - communicate via email where everything is documented and you can take some time to phrase your next response without being pressured in a face-to-face meeting or a phone conversation. When they are pressing you about your lease or have rejected your idea or a reduction or a grace period, give them time to think about it, then let them know that without a reduction in revenue, you do not think your business is viable anymore and you'll have to close up shop.

Now if your store is in a highly sought-after area and the economy is sound, it's quite likely the landlord will tell you something equivalent to not letting the door hit you on the way out. They can get you moved out, spend a little money on touch ups to the space, and have new clients moving in next week.

However if this is during a time of pandemic, war, hurricane disaster or financial crisis etc, the landlord will probably want to see you survive, as some money from you is better than an empty building. Most likely after a few rounds of negotiation, they will agree to a reduction. You will also need to agree about other details such as payback or arrears and any interest, but once you've got them to agree to let you stay at a reduced rate, the rest of it will be significantly easier to haggle.

Have a rainy day fund that is secure from business creditors and bankruptcy

Chapter 7:

Thinking Outside the Box

The best thing to remember is that in times of crisis, there are always other routes to take to save money and buy your business more time to recover. These ideas are just a few things that I have tried and succeeded with, or considered after seeing others have success with them.

- **Sublease some of your location or office space:** There are tons of businesses that share space. Some are complementary businesses, but even that does not have to be true. But if I was still running my auction business or the used car dealership, I could have rented out space to a service that fixes windshield dings or a place that touches up your paint, or does detail work. A reduction in your lease is always a good thing, and if you can pick the right partner to share your space, you could possibly also be improving both your revenue and theirs by having customers spill over from one side to the other.

- **Change your business from a brick-and-mortar location to online.** We touched on this earlier when we discussed your landlord playing hardball and not letting you out of the lease. It's an option, and some people actually find it to be an improvement over the physical location because it minimizes costs so effectively. A lot of times this is an ego struggle more than anything. If you've owned a building with your company's name on the sign, your picture on the wall, your own office, and all that jazz, it can be tough not to feel like a failure when you're suddenly moving all the office equipment into a storage facility and your new 'Command Central' is the desk in your spare bedroom. But the success of your business is not measured on who has the prettiest office, but rather on who has the most satisfied customers and revenue generated. Would you rather be bleeding $5,000 per month on costs for a beautiful office that is devoid of customers or start working from your home office for $50 per month and be turning a profit while everyone else is just praying to break even?

- **Fixed overheads are never fixed:** Your utilities and suppliers are not robots who are fixed on the "Profit" switch and cannot be reasoned with like normal people. They know that your business is just as human an organization and that you're going to have some months of great success and some months of failure. The purpose here is not to be a beggar and wait until the last minute to let them know you cannot pay your bill for the month. That's not being proactive and that sort of behaviour will play out quickly with businesses that rely on you to make timely payments to pay their own staff, cover their own expenses, and make their own profits. When you come to them asking for help, be transparent. Tell them what the problem is, how you plan to solve it, what you can offer, and what terms you'd like to ask for, as well as how you're planning to make up for the amounts you are not paying in the present. Ask for help and give them an idea of the time frame for when you will need their help. Give them time to think your offer over; don't tell them that you need an answer in the next 24 hours, that's not fair to them. But also deliver a deadline - "Can you give me an answer by Friday?" so that you can make your plans accordingly.

- **Give your staff options:** If you're the type of boss who marches in one Monday morning and fires half of your staff because you can no longer afford to pay their salaries, word will get around quickly and you'll find it increasingly difficult to find quality people who want to come work for you, even in the worst of times. When things start getting tight, make sure you provide your staff with options that can keep them employed, even if it's not at their usual rate of pay. Offer them to work from home if that is an option in your line of business, but tell them it will come at a reduction of hours as well. Some employees might be happier working 25-30 hours a week at home than 40 hours in the office, because of the work-life balance it frees up for them, not to mention not having to get dressed up and make the commute! For others the reduction in hours might be mandatory in the short term, with the promise of putting them back to full time as business picks up. If you cannot achieve your budget reduction through reducing staff hours, you'll have to move into redundancies and start negotiating settlements with employees whose jobs are being made redundant. You can take on these positions yourself or consider using online resources to help with processes that can be automated such as accounting, invoicing, customer relations, etc.

Chapter 8:

A Note on Business During COVID-19

As I type these words, the government of New Zealand is slowly putting our country back to work. We were one of the lucky ones, it seems. With our smaller population spread over a large amount of land, social distancing came more naturally to us than in places like China, US, and Italy. As of May 1, 2020, we had only suffered 20 lives lost from this global pandemic. But that did not make the effect on our businesses any less devastating.

The first lockdowns started on March 14, and they were only reduced a few days ago. That means six weeks of shuttered storefronts and CLOSED signs in the windows. When you're living your business life day to day, six weeks is an eternity. Regardless of where you are or what your business is, it is extremely likely that the COVID-19 pandemic has affected your business. This is a once-in-a century event when it comes to unprecedented conditions and a general downturn of business. While it is not exactly a silver lining, these truths will greatly help you negotiate when it comes to getting your outstanding business bills paid off. I would negotiate very hard for a permanent reduction and arrears to be written off and no interest. Once you go into this territory, there can be legal consequences and you might lose control of the property under your business. This advice is for the most dire of cash flow crises, and you should consult a legal/accounting professional about your lease for specific advice.

In 2008, my landlords agreed to a significant rent reduction and I paid the arrears back in the following years. They very kindly gave this arrangement to me interest free. Once the formal lease period had finished and I was signing a new lease, the market rate was a lot lower and I achieved a significant permanent reduction!

Chapter 9:

Guidelines and To-Do List

Break-even point

Your break-even point is the amount of money you need to generate per month to pay for all your bills. It's the dollar amount you have to make each month in order to pay for all your monthly expenses. Even if you are not running the financial or administrative parts of your business, you should be monitoring the ins and outs constantly to be on top of the situation. Don't wait six weeks for an admin or accountant's report to tell you if the month was good or bad.

Do a budget/cash-flow forecast

A cash-flow forecast will provide you a clear picture of what money is coming in and what money goes out, so you can manage your cash better. You need to know your income and expenses for each and every week. As someone who has long been a long-term planner, it simply blows my mind when people will not plan ahead and use the data that is right in front of them to better understand the trends of their business in particular, and the larger economy in general. Spotting trends and realizing business is slowing down and you need to start saving up for lean times is just one way to make it through recessions. Knowing your numbers is very important. This can help you cut down on extra spending like unneeded staff hours and unexpected bills or projects that can be put off until later.

Payment Arrangements with Suppliers

Ring, or go see your suppliers, and make small weekly payment arrangements with them. Don't wait for them to call you. Identify critical suppliers and keep them sweet. They will be a lot more receptive to taking less money more frequently if you approach them and explain yourself, rather than having to track you down and demand that you pay up. By the same token, if a less valuable supplier is not giving you a chance to reduce your short-term payments, they are a supplier that won't break your back to lose permanently.

Payment Arrangements with Landlord

Ring or go see your landlord and negotiate a cheaper rate for at least 6 months. Remember that if the economy is strong and your business is located in an area that is highly sought after, your bargaining power is going to be significantly reduced. But if times are tight and you've been consistent with your payments in the past, most landlords would rather give you the chance to make it up to them in the future than risk seeing you forced to move out and leave them with an empty suite. That looks bad to people driving by, makes your neighbors antsy that they're next, and it is costly to find a new tenant in tough times.

Purchasing products or services for delayed delivery

Companies go out of business with horrifying quickness when recessions hit, as many of them are operating on shoe-string budgets or just barely easing by month to month without any sort of backup plan or rainy-day fund. When you have contracts that you pay upfront for later delivery, consider whether or not that company is one that might go out of business during such a time. If you think it's a possibility, pull out of the deal and keep your funds close to home. There's nothing worse than paying for a delivery to a company that can't keep its doors open, and folds with your money in its pocket and your supplies nowhere to be found.

Secure a line of credit in advance

Remember that it was the banks that had to get bailed out during the Global Financial Crisis of 2007-2009. Lehman Brothers, founded in 1847, filed for bankruptcy in 2008 and as part of a US government stimulus of $700 billion to buy out the bad loans it had approved. Unfortunately, the tendency of banks to pay that good-will forward has rarely been seen since! If times are tight and you can't pay your bills, banks are going to close your line of credit sooner or later. Stay ahead of the game by calling your friends, family members, or anyone else willing to extend you a line of credit for your business expenses. Don't wait for things to get worse.

Liquidate cash tied up in assets if you have to

Desperate times call for desperate measures, and nothing is more important than having cash in hand for things that are essential purchases at times like these. That Harley Davidson you only ride on Saturdays when the weather is nice? It needs to find a new home. A pleasure boat or sports car or vacation property that you use much more as a status symbol than for its actual purpose? Trust me, if it means that much to you, you can reward yourself with a better one down the line. Don't be so attached to a physical object or your own ego that it sacrifices your ability to do business down the line.

Cut down costs

Have a look at your staffing structure. Do you need to layoff some staff or reduce hours across the board, for example from 40 hours to 20 hours? Think about power usage: you may be paying for heat, air conditioning, computers, and printers when no one is using them. Cut your own paycheck as well. You only need enough money to survive until this crisis is over. You can worry about your profits when you have saved your business.

Know when to quit

Are you going to make a bigger mess if you stay open? No matter how many actions you take or how savvy you are as a business owner, some businesses will fail. Know when it is time to pull the plug. We will cover this in more detail later in the book.

Chapter 10:

Causes of Unexpected Downturns in Business

- Unforeseen political rule changes

- Loss of a major customer

- Loss of key staff member(s)

- Significant or fast increases in competition

- Technological changes

- A Black Swan effect

While you might not know when one of these events is coming, you can still plan ahead to mitigate the damage they inflict. But let's face it, things can get away from you at times. The trick is to survive, thrive, and learn for next time.

Issues can build slowly while you work hard trying to cope with them. The simple fact is that you need to be steering in advance of potential issues. Bad times are going to come, but you can't always know when, how, or for how long. My story is about simply working harder and smarter as the solution.

In times of crises like COVID-19, you are forced to work on your business rather than in the business. The lockdown forces you to stay indoors and reflect on your next move. This is the time to work on your business plan, upskill yourself, and learn new habits. Look at your products, your supplier list, your utilities bills, and see if you can save some money somehow - do a competitive analysis. Learn new ways to analyze your data and see the trends that you might otherwise have been too busy to spend time on.

Chapter 11:

Getting Prepared for the Next Crisis

In the GFC years, I clearly remember how horrible it was being a car auctioneer and showing 60-90 vehicles to only about 5-6 buyers. In the good times (pre-GFC), we would have hundreds of buyers. That sort of downturn in customer volume is catastrophic. I quickly had to restructure this to only drive-through, and show cars that people were there to bid on, which was about 10-15 vehicles. Instantly this felt easier and our costs - like paying the drivers - were reduced. Prior to GFC, for years I had occasionally played devil's advocate and considered what would happen if things changed or there was a war or some natural disaster. So I started thinking of the bigger picture of what can be done to stay alive in business. Here are the steps you can take to prepare yourself for such a time when it invariably rises again.

The Better Business Plan: Sales, Costs, and Efficiencies

Give yourself time to think creatively

Once a week, I would go for a walk up a local hilltop to get some exercise, clear my head, and just let my thoughts wander.

On this particular occasion, I sat under the tree looking at the view, and that's when I decided to change to selling by daily tender versus one weekly auction. It was not entirely an innovative idea, as a similar company in another town was using this model to sell its cars. However, it took a clear mind and being open to giving anything a go, which led me to explore and entertain the concept of selling cars by daily tender.

Well, if your business is almost dead, you might as well try anything to fix it. Tender is a type of paper auction. Tenders enabled me to sell older cars at high volumes cheaply, as it excluded any dealer warranties with New Zealand law. Compared to a weekly auction, changing to tenders meant people could put in offers and buy each day. We did not need to pay for an auctioneer or drivers to drive cars through on the auction night. We found customers changed from hard-dealing, bargain-buyer types who only wanted to steal a deal at auction, to nicer folks who just wanted a nice car today. It was an absolute epiphany and made the business process a lot more of a pleasant experience for everyone involved, not to mention cutting our costs nicely.

The other change we went through, was instead of selling vehicles on behalf of individuals and charging a small commission, we began to purchase vehicles outright and almost doubled our profits on each sale compared to the old commission. We could also buy more cars, increase the selection, and thus increase sales. Without going through the GFC, I doubt I would have made such changes. It kind of forced us to change, and these changes really worked. Sales started going up, costs went down, and our margin doubled. In six months' time, everything changed from doom and gloom back to sunshine and rainbows. We were back.

Making these changes was quite scary. I thought to myself that I always had the option to change back if I noticed something was not working. I even got my key staff member involved. I took him aside one day and asked about his financial situation, and told him that we were cutting back. It would be me and him as the last person standing if we got to that stage. He said he had some savings and that he could sell other stuff if he had to get more cash. He was happy to support me during this transition, and in the end our changes and cutbacks meant I kept most of my staff. That's something not nearly enough people think about during tough times: your staff. Just think how many people are bending over backwards to ensure they are at the job ready to work every day. When times are tight, you owe it to them to give your all to keep them employed as close to normally as possible. People that are loyal and smart and love your business are about the most valuable resource there is.

It was like being on the reality TV show "Survivor". We had outplayed, outwitted, and outlasted many of our competitors who had been forced to close up shop. With the market bouncing back, business was really good again. My point is that I would never have thought that the changes I made in such a horrible time would have led me to semi-retirement on a large catamaran ten years later.

Creating a New Business Plan

You don't have to spend thousands of dollars with an accountant or high-end consultant to do your business plan. In fact, if you're reading this while your business is shuttered during the COVID-19 lockdown, now is a great time to learn some new skills - like how to do a proper business plan all by yourself!

Don't get bogged down in details, keep it simple and get it down on paper so you can start refining it. Accountants and consultants can be good, but can get caught in too many details and miss the bigger picture. Plus, since you're paying them for their services, they're going to want what they produce to be as perfect as possible in order to earn their fees.

You know about your business and industry more than anyone. Now you have the time to do it. When writing a business plan, you will need to review all parts if it (and especially in times of crises) – from income, expenses, marketing, suppliers, products/services, competition to market, economy, technology, etc.

How can you deliver your product/services in a more efficient way to the market and do so better, cheaper, or faster than your competition? Can you reinvent your product or services? These are some of the hard questions you need to think of and address. Think outside the box. For example, can you give up your rent and operate from your garage/home? Can you recreate your service to market it online? With the recent lockdown, most restaurants and cafes are delivering meals to front doors; can you turn your restaurant into a drive-through restaurant? A client of mine started streaming yoga online since she can't continue with her physical classes, and is already making money. Her market size has increased from just a few locals in her hometown to now all over the world! In times of crisis, you need to think creatively and outside the box to stand out from your competition. Your focus needs to be on the bigger picture.

The way we marketed was a big change for us during the GFC. Before it all came crashing down, newspaper and radio ads were the main form of advertisement for the car yard. Well, when we changed our business model from auction to tenders, we started marketing online. Even then, the common use and knowledge of the Internet was only about 8 or 9 years old, and plenty of people were not sold on it being the successor to traditional advertising.

That turned out to be one of the best decisions I made at that time. No longer were we limited to the people who read the local paper or were within distance of the local radio station's transmitter. Suddenly, the phones were ringing from all over the country and selling cars became easy. That decision saved us a lot of money. How are you marketing your business? Can you think of doing it differently now? In the current times, social media like Facebook is quite useful, and yet very few businesses are using it. It is a cheaper option as well. Since you have time on your hands, you can find out what mode of media works for your business, profile your customers, and do a survey to find out how they are finding your type of business. This is the time to invest in yourself and upskill, and to get educated on marketing. If you have not done so in the past, this is a great time to really learn the analytics behind your business.

In addition to writing your business plan, you can construct some customer persona models. This means figuring out who your typical customer is, and designing your marketing and advertising around them. Take details from your previous customers and find common trends that permeate them. Consider things like their age, their gender, where they live, how much money they spend on your business, what products they spend the most money on, are they married, do they have kids? You can create 1-3 models of your typical customer, and use those to design a plan for how you are going to market and advertise to them. If the average age of your customers is in their 20s or 30s, they are probably going to respond well to posts on social media like Instagram and Twitter. If they are over the age of 50, they're more likely to be email readers or people that still like getting phone calls or letters in the mail. The better you know your customers, the more likely you are to be successful at marketing to them and communicating with them the way that they most enjoy being talked to. The more you know about this process, the less money and effort you have to waste taking 'shots in the dark' on how best to appeal to each niche.

Another huge change we made was re-negotiating our lease agreement. The lease/rent had gone up many times in the previous eight years I had been in business and was quite a large part of my fixed expenses. Cashflow was extremely tight and I was only just managing to stay in business by paying only the absolutely necessary bills, so it was time for a chat with the landlords to see if they wanted to help save the business. I drafted an initial email detailing the changes to the business turnover and asked for assistance reducing the rent cost. We still had six years to run on the lease. I sent them a copy of my new budget so they could see what I was paying myself and where other money was going. They then agreed to a meeting and a significant reduction in the monthly outgoing. I sent them ongoing monthly profit reports for the next six months to keep them up to date. After about six months, I was back into a consistent monthly profit and was able to start making payments on the rent arrears. A few years later when the lease expired, I was able to achieve a significant reduction in rent as the overall market values had decreased.

If your business is in trouble during what is perceived as normal economic times, it is easy to blame yourself. However, in times like the ongoing global pandemic, the downturn is outside of your control. It's a once-in-a-lifetime occurrence and you can't take that blame on your shoulders. This means you can start re-negotiating any contracts and fixed commitments to achieve reductions in overhead.

Will the other party like this? No, but if handled properly they will listen, as it is mutually beneficial for you to stay in business and pay them some money rather than no money.

If you go out of business, would a landlord be able to lease the building anyway? Most likely your supplier is in the same boat as you in the downturn, many of their other clients have already gone out of business and they would rather discount their services to help keep doing business with you.

What about staffing costs? Staffing costs are some of the biggest costs for most small-to-medium businesses. Nobody likes making staff redundant. It is a horrible job, very stressful, and causes a lot of sleepless nights. I had to make my key senior staff redundant during the Global Financial Crisis. She was really good and I had great respect for her. It was still difficult to negotiate redundancy pay with her. She played hard ball requesting 8 weeks' pay when I offered 4 weeks. At that stage, I was working my arse off and juggling cashflow trying to pay landlords and other suppliers. She wasn't going to lose $100,000 in a month if she couldn't make the turnover; it was me, the business owner, who was in that particular jam. In the end she did get a good job and went out with 4 weeks' redundancy pay. The lesson I learned was that in times of crisis, it's every man (and woman) for themselves, so you need to do what you need to do to survive.

What is the point of retaining staff when the business can't make any sales? You can't simply pay people to stand around. As I said earlier, making decisions on staff changes like redundancy or reducing hours is very difficult and most of the time you are seen as a heartless business owner. I even had to let go of my girlfriend, who was the salesperson at the time for my business. These are the decisions where you have no choice but to set a firm jaw and pull the trigger; merge the jobs if you can, reduce hours, or get rid of senior staff if the time comes to do that. Draw an organisational structure chart of roles and positions, and brainstorm how services can be delivered with fewer people without compromising the quality of the services. Can you make a couple of expensive people redundant and roll their job into yours, or junior staff? Instead of 3-4 junior staff, I prefer to employ a couple of more expensive ones that can do everything, and can train other people when the time comes. Can you outsource some work like admin?

Chapter 12:

Pausing and Restarting in COVID-19

It is considerably ironic that when I started this book, I had no clue what the coronavirus was or what it meant. A few folks in Wuhan, China, were coming down sick. I couldn't find Wuhan on a map and whatever it was, it was taking place thousands of miles away from New Zealand. The emphasis of this book was going to be on how the GFC affected me and my business, and how to keep the next recession from putting your business at the same type of risk. Little did I know that the next global financial crisis would spring to life as I was writing about getting ready for it!

The quarantine has forced many businesses to press the "pause" button, something that has never occurred globally in any of our lifetimes. Every business on every level of society has been affected by this pandemic in some way, because all businesses are related and rely on each other in some form or fashion. This isn't a downturn in real estate or bank loans or a plunge in the price of crude oil. This is an event that has forced us all to get home, stay home, be safe, and have patience. Those are some of the most difficult things for business owners to do. We would rather work 20 hours a day to make $100 of sales than be told we have to close our stores, stay inside, and not go back to work this Monday, or next Monday, or anytime in the near future. But this is not your fault and your business is not going to fail if you take the proper steps to salvage things now. We're not hitting the eject button - assuming you're old enough to remember what that looked like on a cassette player or VCR - we are just pressing pause and getting ready for your upcoming resurgence. Here are the essential steps to making sure you survive this period of inactivity.

- Stop the cashflow bleed

- If some level of turnover still exists, then it's a matter of cutting back on your expenses

- Assess your financial ability: What can you afford?

- For ongoing updated advice on the coronavirus and your business, please subscribe to my website www.peterrollo.biz

- Simply stop if that's your last option, there is no shame in that. Are you going to do more damage to your financials by being in business?

Chapter 13:

What Happens to your Business After the Crisis?

Be ready for a boom after a few years, when confidence and demand bounce back in the economy. If you have stayed in business, you will have a head start on all your competition. This is where you can make significant profits. You will be able to hire better staff than ever before. There will be the capacity to get things done again. Suppliers will be keen, helpful, and attentive. You will soon notice your bank balances going up. This is a good time to start saving up for the next rainy days.

Chapter 14:

Business Plan - Guidelines and To-Do List

Invest in yourself first

Despite being in a crisis, take time out to exercise and breathe. This enables you to creatively think about your problems and options and look after yourself. Avoid alcohol and drugs and stimulants such as caffeine. You need to win the long game with your health.

**Challenge your current business model.
Can you create something better?**

Examples:

- Change in structure - restaurants delivering meals to homes or becoming drive-through/take-away establishments.

- My uncle had a chainsaw and mower sales and repair shop. Nowadays major department stores sell the gear, undercutting him. So my idea for his business was to drop retail sales and focus on the repair market.

- You have to try different strategies to get different outcomes. Doing the same thing results in the same outcomes. So think outside the box. Be creative and bold to give a go to new ideas or try something different. You will soon find out that 9 out of 10 decisions will be good ones. Doing nothing is accepting the status quo.

Marketing

- Review your marketing spend. If you have not tried the latest and newest marketing options, it is now time to learn. This could mean creating a business page on Facebook, videos for a YouTube channel, or a blog for people to follow.

- Run live seminars or write *'how to guides'* for your industry. These activities have been a big long boom in the last ten years. Maybe your business has been able to be successful with little or bad marketing and with an average sales process. Now is the time to be very proactive to create demand for your business, and grab every potential sale by the collar and not let go.

- Set up systems to monitor which marketing spend works. They say 50% is wasted so find that waste. And yes with slow sales now, you have time to do all of this!

Leases/ Rent – Renegotiate

- Sublease some of your location or office space.

- Change your business space from bricks and mortar to online only from your garage or home office.

	Review your staffing structure • Can you cut down hours? • Can you merge jobs together? • Can you use contractors instead of a permanent staff?
	Do your budget/cash flow Refer to the section above for budget/cash flow template

Chapter 15:

Conclusion

If you have ever read Aesop's fables, you might recall the tale of the Grasshopper and the Ant. The Grasshopper is a creature of summer and is living for the moment, much like some businesses do in boom times; spending money to grow, grow, grow as the revenues roll in. Meanwhile the Ant, much like the Stark family from "Game of Thrones" realizes that winter is coming soon, and that he needs to work hard to save and save and save in order to survive the coming storm. When winter arrives, the ant is prepared and is able to pull through by rationing. The grasshopper does none of the same preparation work and is on the verge of starvation once winter comes. The lesson is an obvious one, and as timely in 2020 as it was when Aesop penned it more than 3,000 years earlier. The only way to survive the inevitable down times, crises, and even once-in-a-lifetime global pandemics, is to prepare in the long term and survive in the short term.

Outside of saving every possible penny you can, ensure that when things start to go south, you start implementing your survival mode resources including keeping lots of cash on hand, maximizing your billing cycles, arranging different payment structures with your suppliers, and staying one step ahead of the dominos before they fall. When you work hard at pivoting your business and holding on through the toughest of times, you may surprise yourself on what you can achieve. If you had told me in 2008 that 12 years later I'd be living mortgage free in a house I love and embarking on a trip around the world on my own catamaran, I would have had you checked into a mental hospital!

Remember, the grasshopper mentality might have you living it up in the moment, but when you plan like the ant, your business will survive the next black swan event and emerge even stronger. If I can do it, then you can too.

Dedicated to

Blair Phelps, one of my best staff member/friends who was tragically
killed in a motorcycle accident

My parents, Harold and Christine Rollo

Special thanks to

Yogeeta Devi, co-author, accountant and supportive partner

Skye Temara, whose hard work during the 2008 GFC and absolute faith and loyalty to me as her employer for 14 years is humbling

Get in touch

For further business advice and accounting and for a free downloadable and printable PDF to-do list based on the book, visit www.peterrollo.biz

Interested in sailing and traveling around the world? Follow us on YouTube: search Peter Rollo

Disclaimer: The information provided in this book does not constitute legal, tax or accounting advice, but is designed to provide general information relating to business and commerce. Peter Rollo content, information products and services are not a substitute for obtaining the advice of a competent professional, for example a licensed attorney, law firm, accountant or financial adviser that is specific to your business.